MW00625090

Dear
2021

Dear 2021

21
letters for 2021

LISSEDIA BATISTA-GONZALEZ

Copyright © 2022 by Lissedia Batista

All rights reserved. No part of this publication may be reproduced,
stored or transmitted in any form or by any means, electronic, mechanical,
photocopying, recording, scanning, or otherwise without written
permission from the publisher. It is illegal to copy this book, post it
to a website, or distribute it by any other means without permission.

Lissedia Batista asserts the moral right to be identified as the author
of this work.

Lissedia Batista has no responsibility for the persistence or accuracy of
URLs for external or third-party Internet Websites referred to in this
publication and does not guarantee that any content on such Websites is,
or will remain, accurate or appropriate.

Designations used by companies to distinguish their products are often
claimed as trademarks. All brand names and product names used in this
book and on its cover are trade names, service marks, trademarks and
registered trademarks of their respective owners. The publishers and the
book are not associated with any product or vendor mentioned in this book.
None of the companies referenced within the book have endorsed the book.

The authors grants Lissedia Batista the first publication rights for
publication in Dear 2021: 21 Letters for 2021.

First edition

This book was professionally typeset on Reedsy. Find out more at reedsy.com

If you wrote a letter for this book, thought about writing a letter but couldn't get through it, read a single letter but never pick it up again, finish the whole book in one sitting or simply purchased it in support, I dedicate this book to you.

Thank you

CONTENTS

ANOTHER YEAR, MORE OF THE SAME.

letter 1

Dear 2021,

Our relationship reminds me of the lyrics in that Katy Perry song, Hot and Cold. If I had to describe it, that's exactly how I would do it. The whole time we were together felt like a rollercoaster of emotions with thrilling highs and disappointing lows.

In your efforts to woo me when you first arrived, you presented yourself as our savior. You gave me things to look forward to and painted me a great future ahead. You gave me something I had been missing and craving since last year. Hope. I was happy in this new relationship you and I were starting. I was hopeful and blinded by your love. Even though you brought us an insurrection, talks of impeachment, and crazy Covid-19 mandates, I ignored the red flags because I was determined to be selfish this year and focus on my family and me. Somehow, I found a way to feel safe and happy with you.

Though February is mostly a blur because I was busy working on my book project, I can see you were trying your best to keep me happy. At work, we were allowed to keep our student groups every day rather than that annoying, alternating schedule the system established months prior. Things were settling in the classroom, and it started to feel safe enough that I had my daughter return to the school building. It felt like things were "going back to normal," and I was happy to have some control over that part of my life.

In March, I became a self-published author. Interviews, Pop-Ups, and book promotion events took up most of my time that month. I was basking in the glory of the project's attention and the support from family and friends, too busy to notice the things that imposter syndrome had rudely come and crashed the party.

The mom, wife, daughter, sister, and teacher struggled to stay relevant and active. Each one of us with a bag full of worries, heartaches, and fears. Each fighting to keep it together and pretend that it was all good. All of my layers were struggling to stay intact and in place. Jenga pieces ready to tumble at any time. I looked to you for help, but your solutions only caused me more problems down the road.

You see, 2021, in my quest to find normalcy, to feel good—to ignore the pain that was slowly growing and eating me away—a pain I did not understand, I found a temporary solution to my pain, something that made me happy. I started online shopping. It felt fulfilling and powerful, giving me a rush I could not explain. It felt good. So I did it often. Online shopping became my therapy in a world where finding a therapist was impossible—and browsing Amazon was my daily medicine. I started hiding boxes from my husband, but the boxes eventually piled up, and the financial hole I dug myself was too big for him not to notice. I created a deep financial hole, and we now have to recover from it together.

You must have noticed my struggle because you took it easy on me in the summertime, at least for a while. Thank you for that. You made it possible for us to have some fun. The kids were active; dance, sports, and mini-vacations took most of our time. I even got to hang out and see my friends again. But one thing I can say about you is that you are consistent. You got bored quickly. That's about the time when my 7-year-old was diagnosed with Alopecia Areata. How dare you? Did you think that was funny? Well, we are not laughing!

The rest of the year, I was cautious. You had become predictable in a way, and I was waiting for you to strike again so I could be ready. I wasn't surprised when you ruined our holiday by bringing Covid home. Instead, I sat down and thought about our time together. It was the perfect time to reflect.

I realized that maybe you weren't so bad after all. You were trying to make me stronger. A sort of endurance test if you must. Something I could not see then but can appreciate now. A challenge where I became a better teacher, wife, and mom. So, as I am writing these last lines to you, I thank you for the highs and the lows because I would not have been able to grow without them.

I won't miss you, but I promise I'll remember you forever.

The year after the pandemic. An unforgettable one.

Adios 2021,
LBG

letter 2

Dear 2021

What can I say? You have been full of blessings.

After everything that happened with 2020, I decided to take it easy this year and let you and me take things slow. I knew I had to approach you differently. With Covid hitting so hard, schools closed, and my kids dealing with all the craziness, I had to make changes.

I decided to work the night shift to teach the boys in the morning and still make money during this whole ordeal. It did not feel safe to have them return to the classroom just yet, and with them working remotely, I needed to make sure that I was around to help them with their schoolwork. It was crazy time, but the boys needed me and I needed the crazy to make sense, at least to them. I would go to work at 8 pm, come out at 8 am and shift from my role of supervisor to teacher's assistant to help the boys with their homework, monitor speech therapy, and manage Noah's tantrums.

The boys had a hard time adapting to this new normal, and honestly, so did I. So, when Noah kept throwing the iPad in frustration, I knew that we all needed a change. That's when I decided to visit my sister in Texas and change the scenery. Why not? Right? It's not like things were all that great around here. So, I did what my family needed. I took a leave of absence from work and told my boyfriend I was testing the waters to see what else was out there for us.

I packed my stuff, bought three flights to Texas, and we have not been back to New York since.

It wasn't an easy decision, but it was the right decision for us.

I stayed with my sister for a while, but we didn't want to overstay our welcome. So, I started to look for an apartment a couple of months in, while my boyfriend did what needed to be done to meet me here. We were well on the way to our new life. Neither of us had jobs and our savings were running out quickly, but we were happier than we had been in a very long time.

2021, you had me work at what felt like a million jobs! I was losing faith quickly, as I often do when things don't go my way quickly. "All in God's time," my sister would say. And she was right because, after a while, I finally got a job at Chick-fil-A. It did not last long, but I will always be grateful for all the lessons I learned there. After I left, I found a job at a daycare center. I liked it because it had a more flexible schedule for me and the kid's school, and things started to feel better. The boys were learning so many things, and the teachers loved them. That alone made the initial struggle worth it. My kids were finally starting to settle in their new home and the doubts that we initially had about moving out of New York started to disappear.

Of course, 2021, you saw us happy and decided that it was time to test our patience again. I began to see things I did not like. There was a lot of rule-breaking at the day care center. After a month or two, I knew this was a sinking ship, things were rocky and everyone kept quitting, so I too had to do the best thing for my family, I needed to leave and the day they forgot to pay me, was the day I walked out.

It felt like a punch to the stomach. I started to question the move, and this is when you decided to mix things up. On my birthday, in May, you chose to surprise us with the fantastic news that we were expecting. I was pregnant with my third child. I was as nervous as I was excited, but we knew this was a gift from God.

Three months into the pregnancy, I got Covid. Luckily, I didn't even know I had it! My boyfriend, on the other hand, was not so lucky. He had all the symptoms, and I felt helpless not to take the pain away.

I thank God that pregnancy has been different this time around. Because this is a small town and Covid has not affected us much, I can enjoy my pregnancy without any anxiety or worry that Covid can affect my baby or me. If I had stayed in New York, I do not think it would be the same way.

Thank you for that 2021! It is because of you that I have what I have today. You pushed me to make this move, helped me along the way, and taught me that the essential thing in life is my family. That humility will take me further in life than I thought and that I am stronger than I ever imagined. You have taught me that we don't need much to live a happy life. I just need my kids, my partner, and my rescue dog.

So, 2021, you have been one incredible year no matter the obstacles you presented me with. You humbled my heart. You made me a better person.

Thank you, I will never forget you.

I am so excited about my next adventure ... Here I come 2022!

Shirley D.
Mother of two, soon to be three

letter 3

Dear 2021,

I could start by telling you that you have been the worst year that I've ever had the displeasure of experiencing. But there was so much more to you. I think it's just that you have been a bad guest. I invited you and welcomed you, but you decided to come with baggage. And not the type I wanted to help you unpack. I mean, I was already dealing with a lot from the previous year as a health professional and all I wanted was to leave all of it behind, but you carried an epidemic with you from the prior year. Next time bring wine, flowers, or chocolate, not a pandemic.

Why would you show up with such an intrusive travel companion? You should have left him behind. I'm sure you have seen the news, and you knew exactly what you were doing. But just in case no one has dared to tell you yet, let me just remind you of a couple of things your travel partner has done in the past.

Covid-19, your precious friend, was a total terror! A lethal pandemic that changed the lives of many innocent people. It created an unbearable situation for people in my field. Heartbreaking situations where I saw people in my line of duty at the hospital dying daily from left to right since the outbreak of the disease.

I do not want to seem bitter, but the reality is that I am. Last year was too much, and this year, there was a lot of the same. Everything has continued to be a disaster. Families are still unable to gather, businesses remain closed, and schools were partially opened but were a contagious trap. And yes, I know that we emerged as heroes, with essential service providers, doctors, paramedics, and nurses coming to the forefront to stop the spread of your selfish friend behind the disease. I know I should count my blessings and be more positive. Still, the reality is that it is complicated to do that, especially after the solution you presented continued to cause trouble and people lost their jobs. Two words for you: vaccine mandates.

When do you think all of this will be done? You have some of the blame now. You have allowed coronavirus to continue to spread globally, as if 2020 was not enough! It used YOU to continue to cause the deaths of thousands of innocent people. And you let it. In April 2021, you allowed him to get too close to me and disrespect my home. You should have kept it in check and explained that he should not have come for my family. I had to isolate myself for over three weeks. I wasn't feeling like myself; I felt guilty for letting you in my life. I cried every night, my pillow never dried up. It's crazy the number of things that go through your head when you are in isolation. Loneliness is a crazy beast. But I reminded myself to pray every night as I was battling your unwanted friend and the unwanted thoughts in my head. I was ready for you to be gone. I apologize if I do not seem sad that you are leaving. If it seems that I am eager, it's because I am. You were a heartbreaker.

2021, even though you intended to break me, I'm still standing and feel stronger than ever. As bad as it sounds, I must thank you, but first, I thank the lord above for allowing me and blessing me after 17 years to be a mother of my third child (baby coming in June 2022. **It's god's blessing** after all the stress and uncomfortable daily living. I can already tell that 2022 will be my best friend.

2021 thank you for everything you have done, **good and bad**!

Until never 2021,

Kelcia Peralta

Nursing Assistant soon to be Registered Nurse to continue helping others.

.

letter 4

Dear 2021,

I am still here. I'm standing! Looking back at the obstacles I faced during your time here, I can now call myself a warrior! When I couldn't run, I walked. When I couldn't walk, I crawled. Whatever it took to keep moving. I did not give up. As a first-year teacher amid Covid, I did not know what to expect in the classroom. I was counting on you to bring order, healing, and celebration. Instead, I faced chaos, restlessness, and sleepless nights.

I imagined a classroom full of color, character, and bright minds ready to learn, perform and thrive. But I was met instead with challenges, delays, and face masks! Where I wanted to see smiles when my students understood a concept or solved a problem independently, all I could see were tired eyes and furrowed brows. Warmth was at a far reach as I couldn't connect with my students with a hug, rather a handshake as if we had just struck a business deal. Students require close contact in a special education setting to build a trusting relationship and affirm that trust. Instead of going home to plan lessons, I spent hours planning creative ways to ease their fears and believe in the new "normal" before diving into the curriculum. Where I imagined planning for one grade, I quickly found out I was bridging three! You created a real mess for schools with your vaccine mandates and staff shortage.

2021, I counted on you to bring back the joy and love for learning that we all lost a year ago. I counted on you to create space for all of us to act on the lessons of courage, triumph, and appreciation that 2020 forced us to build. I counted on you to enable growth and live out the teaching dreams I've had for as long as I could remember, but you did not understand the assignment!

Your energy was so negative that when I took our classroom's fishes home for Christmas break ... they all died!

But again, I did not give up, my students still love me, the classroom, and learning, and I bought more fishies.

Oh! How can I forget? I met someone who I now know will be a part of my life forever. Shoutout to my classroom para!

Sincerely,
A new teacher from the Bx

letter 5

Dear 2021,

I'm sure you've been told many times that you were meant to be better than the last. I will be no exception. I had big plans for you, and I was able to accomplish most of them for the most part but you also opened up a window into a truth I had long kept under shut.

You started off great! I had a new job and was glad I was finally out of my old situation. I felt like I could breathe again; in a career where I no longer felt joy, I fell in love with what I do all over again. So, when you arrived, I was filled with a sense of wonder that I hadn't felt in some time. I finally felt like I was in control of at least one aspect of my life, and I was happy for that. Grateful even.

In basking in my newfound glory, in late spring, I made a „Summer Bucket List," which I vowed to complete during the summer season (hence the name). The list was filled with places and experiences I would finish by the end of summer. Restaurants, museums, parks, art exhibits, rooftop bars and other things I saw on social media but now wanted to experience beyond the double tapping of the screen on my phone. All the fun things I could not do last year because of Covid, I now wanted to experience with you. You gave me something to look forward to, and I thank you for that. But at the same time, you took some of the fun away. While the list was something exciting, it also made me feel empty.

I realized I would have to do all these fun things alone for the most part. But I refused to continue to use that as an excuse to miss out on all these opportunities. I told myself I needed to have the best summer experience. The truth is, I've never been like most people. I don't have a group of friends, cliques, or a squad. I don't know; let's blame it on my social anxiety and the fact that I consider myself an introvert. My best and closest friend is my sister, who is often busy with her career, family, and bustling social life. I don't feel close to many of my friends anymore. Some have moved away, gotten married, and become parents. They are busy with responsibilities I cannot relate to. We are on different paths of our lives, so things have changed.

But 2021, I had been using the excuse of „everyone is so busy" and „there's no one to go with" for so long that I missed out on many things. Things I've wanted to do and try for what feels like a lifetime. I realized that as awesome as it would have been to experience these things with a loved one, I had to be okay with going on these adventures on my own because life isn't waiting for me. Also, who knows, maybe I could make new friend or meet a new guy while out there since I was flirting with the idea of getting back in the dating pool again.

By the end of August, I had completed most of my list and even dared to add a new item, dating. I had been putting it off for some time, but I told myself I was older and wiser, and I would take it one day at a time. I started by downloading a dating app. One week later, I set up my profile, and a week after that, I started messaging. I met a couple of guys and went on a couple of dates. I soon realized it would take some time to meet a good match, but I was glad for the progress

I had made since my last relationship and since starting therapy. Therapy helped keep me calm and recognize when things just didn't serve me. It helped me recognize when to walk away. So, thank you 2021, for showing me how much I have grown.

In early September, I met a guy I wasn't sure about at first, but we have grown closer over time. We have good conversations, he is kind and funny, and even though we've been together a short time, I can tell this is probably the healthiest relationship I have ever been in. I'm glad for my work and trust I can tell the difference. We had a great few months and had some awesome plans for the end-of-year holidays. But just when I thought 2021 year was the best, everything went to shit when I got Covid three days before Christmas.

Funny joke 2021, except it wasn't. It was the most wonderful time of the year, but not for me! How could this happen? Why now? I love Christmas, I had been planning for weeks. I work at a hospital and commute to and from work on a bus and train, but no, this was the time I got Covid? It was a cruel move on your part, but as my family and I count down on my last day of quarantine and into the new year, I remember all the fun we had and all the things we did, want to say thanks for the memories. I know you did the best you could.

Goodbye 2021, you are truly one for the books.

A

letter 6

Dear 2021,

Where do I start? I know being in college is supposed to be some big self-discovery of who you are and what you want to do and that alone is a lot for my "under-developed mind," as my psychology college professors love to point out. But then you throw in a worsening pandemic and the most significant decline in mental health on earth, in my opinion, of course, and things only get rockier.

You took a lot from me 2021, and I mean A LOT. My good or at least what I thought was good mental health standing, confidence, adventure, happiness, my four-years-long-supposed-to-be-a-Disney-princess-relationship, and my sanity. If that didn't sound bad enough, whilst barely keeping my own boat from sinking, I somehow managed to be in charge of 30 emotional, lost, and havoc-creating 17- to 19-year-old freshmen girls who can't figure out how to do their laundry let alone remember to row their own boats to stay afloat in life. I love my job.

No, but seriously, I do, ... sometimes. But I'd love to talk to the person who thought it was a great idea to ask 12 19- to 22-year-old college students to be responsible for 300 other college students. I know what you're thinking, "It can't be that hard, they're adults." Wouldn't I love that to be the truth. What were you thinking? Leaving me to deal with situations no one my age should be made responsible for. Suicide attempts, sexual harassment. Bias incidents based on sexuality and race.

Physical assaults and relationship violence. At least 2020 only gave me underage drinking and smoking weed, talk about trying to one up.

Hysterically crying with heavy breathing and snot included in the package and having to answer frantic knocks at your door to respond and help someone else's crisis when you're quite literally in the middle of yours is a different level of mind fuck. I wonder how I paraphrase that skill to put on my resume. But what can I say 2021, at least you are consistent.

When people told me not to go into college with a relationship, they should've added "because it'll crumble in front of you while your mind is sounding alarms at your constant feeling of not being okay while in a pandemic :)" on the list of reasons why. No one tells you how bad a falling out with your high school sweetheart is gonna feel. But if we're sticking to the trend, just add it to the several other knives sitting in my chest. After lots of crying, throwing things at my wall (that I ended up having to replace) and shutting myself in my room with barely enough food or sunlight to live, I've come to a conclusion.

I forgive you, 2021. For all the anxiety, tears, heartbreak, anger, phone calls to my mom where I told her "I'm not gonna make it." For taking papa away from us, away from me, crying on my bathroom floor, wishing I was home—wishing I was happy, and middle-of-the-night binge eats. All of it. I'm on the other side now. The side with learning how to date as a 21-year-old versus as a 16-year-old (which is just as fun as it is complicated). The side where I'm recognized for the hard work and I feel good about putting in the effort. The side where I learned my boundaries and stopped being scared to demand people to respect them. The side where I choose to live in the moment because adulting is soon approaching. The side where I can happily talk about the best memories I have with papa without being sad. The side where I realize my body doesn't disqualify me from being deserving of love. The side where I ask myself, "What do you have to lose in trying, or going?" The side where I allowed my self-awareness to get help for what I was feeling instead of sitting in it. The side where I can play my music and dance and sing and scream across my room as loud as I can without thinking if people are listening. The side where I pursue what I'm passionate about wholeheartedly and not only "what makes the most logical sense." The side where I'm happy.

If my lesson from you was to be that anything, and I mean ANYTHING, can be taken from you at any time, I guess you can say you taught me to stop being scared of living.

I wasn't thrilled to make your acquaintance but so happy that you're gone.

Signed,
Nina exhausted college student

letter 7

Dear 2021,

Adios and good riddance!

Wow! How do I forgive and forget you and your crazy roller coaster!

2021 you were an exciting year for me, my family, and my business!

Let's start with the very first month of the year! Boy did the year start strong for me and my business! Things were moving gracefully, and we had work, but on January 10th, I got the call that would make my heart race and my business owner's mindset spark! We finally got the call that we had been waiting for! We were taking over the full cleaning operations for our subcontracting company! We won the race!! Yay!

That was so exciting! It was our time to shine and staff up! We started our first full-day shift on January 17th. Things for me got really fast-paced as had to manage more people, a business, and my family all in a day's process! I was excited, but I was very nervous and overwhelmed. I was considering closing the business because I felt like it wasn't going anywhere, but this really showed me that things happen when they are meant to, not when you want them to.

Let's fast forward to May 25th! Yay! Another location offer! That was even more exciting and unexpected. From the looks of it we were doing pretty good, and we had just gotten an offer to work at JFK Airport in the branch located there. Without any hesitation or fear, I jumped at the offer!

Who would say no to growth? Not me for sure! One thing though was, that I had no staff! No one to work the afternoon cleaning shift. That meant I would have to put in a lot of the work and effort into this location personally until I got some workers. I needed to think of a plan, and I had to do it fast. I decided I would transfer staff from bp to JFK. People who could actually work and pull us through until we got it together. It was a bumpy start, but we got it going.

Three weeks later, the most unexpected call of my life came: We got Newark airport! Wow, 2021! Location #3, you really outdid yourself. This one was definitely a surprise. I was not expecting this at all! Again, we needed to figure out how we would get the staff that could travel daily to and from Jersey! My heart was racing! I literally cried tears of joy! I had to cut my tears short and start working on a game plan. I knew I had to sacrifice my kids and myself a little so that we could make this work. I did everything in my power, but I am only human, and things Jersey started extremely rough. I could barely enjoy the little things anymore, like drinking a cup of coffee without interruptions. I could never get a day off without having my team constantly calling me.

I was so stressed and overwhelmed, but I knew I had to stay focused because this was just the beginning. This was what I had prayed for in the past, and you, the one I least expected, were the one who finally gave it to me.

On December 17th, I was sitting in my mom's living room when I got a group text from another team that worked alongside us, stating that they had lost their contract and that now my team was the main cleaning team. I screamed at the top of my lungs of joy, and no one understood what was going on until I screamed, "WE GOT THE CONTRACT

AT NEWARK!" My mom was so happy, and I called my team to give them the great news. Sheesh, the next few days really kicked out backward! We had to work 18 hour shifts to meet the demand of work! I was there every day of the week due to the short number of staff I had on my team. We needed more people PRONTO!

It's one thing to pray for something and think that you are ready for it, but when reality hits, you have to be ready to give a lot and give up a lot. I wasn't going to let my team down. Now that we got what we wanted, we weren't about to lose it.

2021, by far, you were my year of growth for my business and a year of challenges for my family. Because of all the blessings you sent my way, I had to take some of the focus from them in order to focus my time and energy on my now-booming business. It wasn't all fun. I had some of my most trusted people backstab me and steal from me. I learned a lot, I cried a lot, but most importantly, I grew as a woman and a small business owner.

Thank you for teaching me to count my blessings and never show any fear. This is the game of the strong, and the stronger always survive! It's always a game of survival.

Thank you for helping me grow and allowing me to become the person I am slowly becoming, every day was a learning opportunity next to you, and I am thankful for that.

Safe travels 2021,
A strong and independent small (but not so small)
business owner

letter 8

Dear 2021,

As an administrator, I tell you that you created a real mess for me. So, when I say, "It's not you, it's me," it's because I don't want to hurt your feelings too much. Umm ... no, it's best that we are honest with each other, IT'S NOT ME, IT'S YOU! Please do take it personally for disappointing me so much.

At first, I had high hopes for us, I was even looking forward to us. I was hoping for a new reality, both at work and outside of it, but your actions and behavior started to send negative signals as time went on. Instead of helping me solve problems, you caused new ones. You created a mess of my personal and professional life during our time together by making it impossible for me to do my job well.

What were you thinking? The more I think about it, the more confident I am in my decision to call it quits with you.

I am tired of hiding behind a mask. I am tired of the bruises that the constant hand washing and scrubbing have caused my hands. I'm done running to get tested each time I have a mild headache, feel tired, or have an achy throat. Do you know that my nose has been swabbed over 25 times in our time together?! That is no way to live, and I can't take the abuse anymore! I want my life back. I want normalcy. I hate this damn mask. I want to see the faces of those I work with; my teachers, my kids, and clearly, staying with you won't bring me what I want.

I consider myself a forgiving person, but the troubles you have caused us are unforgivable. Our mental health was at an all-time low; closed classrooms, quarantine, and staff shortages were not something I had envisioned for our time together.

Nevertheless, I thank you because I witnessed my teachers rise to the challenge. Become warriors who ensured that our school ran smoothly in the middle of the chaos you had unleashed. We learned to be resilient.

I have nothing more to say to you.

I respectfully say GOODBYE!

Hope you have NOT such a good life very far away from me.

Extremely Sincerely,
The Admin in Me

letter 9

Dear 2021,

I wanted to catch up with you before all the festivities started and you had to embark on a new journey away from us into the depths of our memories. You see 2021, you were an emotional rollercoaster that many did not survive and others could barely get out of. With you in power, mental health issues were at an all-time high. I know your hands were busy, and you, at no fault of your own, maybe thought it was necessary to focus your attention on other pressing issues. But let me tell you that you dropped the ball on this one. You failed many people, and with the topic of depression and suicidal thoughts hitting so close to home, I am here to ask you, what the fuck were you thinking?

I sit here writing this letter and telling myself that it wasn't all your fault, but the truth is that you were the one here, and I have a lot of questions. 2021, Are you proud of yourself? Did you really have to drive him that close to the edge of his existence?

I hope you know that everything you did to him was uncalled for. That was a shitty move on your part, playing a game with a person's life, because the man felt suffocated and ready to let go. In his efforts to find help, he confessed to having been struggling for years, but somehow, something about you was making things worst. You somehow kept on dumping on his already deep sea of troubles. By pushing this issue aside and making it impossible to find professional help, you pushed him so far that he was ready to give it all up.

A PLAN 2021!

A Fucking PLAN.

He was slowly drowning, and I, also struggling to stay afloat in my own way, dealing with every other part of my life; trying to keep the house running, the family happy, and seeking self-validation, almost did not notice his struggle. I almost lost him.

Did you not think about the aftermath? Were you ready to take responsibility? To take care of the family and me, everything he would have left behind? Did you have to make it that hard to find therapy for someone desperately seeking it? What was your plan? What IS your problem? Are you GOD to toy with someone's emotions that way? Did you think about how I was feeling every time I had to pretend to go up to our room to check on random made-up excuses just to make sure he was still there, breathing, grumpy, alive?

Did you think about me? Me? Your partner in crime this year.

Did you think about the kids?

The trauma?

The empty space his absence would have left behind? Would you have given me a hand or shoulder to cry on? Probably not! Seein' that you are packing and ready to go.

Was it fun seeing our struggle as a couple? Were you really that absorbed in other things that you failed to realize the pain and hurt some were feeling? Or were you just simply testing us?

I kept waiting for you to feel sorry, pay attention, and notice the tears, stress, and fear. But I never seemed to get your attention. DO I HAVE IT NOW?

I was terrified and still am because this is part of our lives now. It is something we have to live with every single day. It is our reality, and we now have to deal with it in the best way possible. But you deserve the truth. You deserve an ear full. I hate you for all of that and cannot wait for you to be gone. You did us wrong, and though I understand that you eventually tried to turn yourself around, the trust is gone. The fear has already been deep-rooted. And I am glad that we are parting ways.

Nonetheless, thank you for showing me that I need to be alert and that I cannot always assume that others are happy and content with life. And thank you for teaching me to be careful when I speak to others and to be present when they need to talk. I may not have all the answers and solutions to the problem, but at least I will be staying while you are leaving like a coward.

Thanks for nothing.

Goodbye,
A scared and worried wife

letter 10

Dear 2021,

Wow, power must be nice, huh?

How'd it feel to tear down the brick walls I stacked between the extra layers of cement I worked so hard to build up all on my own, year after year? I'd scrubbed my life clean only to have to hide my pain under a mask. Although it didn't hide the tears in my eyes, it hid the redness of my face as I cried that one morning when I accidentally came across my old heroine, my savior and drug of choice: heroin.

I spotted her, untouched, in her beautiful tiny clear bag, with her usual companion, a short cut-up straw that I used to use to snort through in my amateur days.

2021, I was fine before you came along. At that moment, you reminded me of the first time I shoved a needleful of what looked like dirty water into my vein and how the last thing I saw was my white, unbrushed hairy Maltese standing on the floor with his head tilted to the left as I fell over to my right, landing on my bed. When I found that bag, all I wanted was to taste it. All I longed for was the bitterness on my tongue more than I did any of the air this mask covering my face kept from my oxygen-deprived lungs. After opening the bag, I did something I regret.

I closed it and ran out of my room in tears. I didn't use that day, and I don't plan to. With the support of someone I love and who has been there for me through thick and thin, it was out of my possession that same day. My knees never stopped trembling, and my eyes were a continuous waterfall. However, I'm proud to say I'm eight years sober and still going strong. I won't say I don't miss it because I am an addict, I will always be an addict, but I will say that I'm an addict that has persevered and will remember these small wins when times get hard.

That is a valuable lesson I learned, thanks to you. So, thank you.

Nikki

Taking your own life. Interesting expression. Taking it from who? Once it's over, it's not you who'll miss it. Your own death is something that happens to everybody else. Your life is not your own. Keep your hands off it!
- Sherlock Holmes

letter 11

"5 ... 4 ... 3 ... 2 ... 1 ... HAPPY NEW YEAR!"

Is it really?

Maybe because we're not writing our date ending with the infamous 2 0? I won't get too much into that, so I'll let you be the judge of the year after we have this brief discussion. By the way, is it ok if I call you Venti? Speaking of, let me call my mom since it's already 12:00 am and it may be my ... wait let me not jump to conclusions yet, Venti, I don't want to spoil it for the rest. I'm glad you're taking the time to hear me out. I'm known for keeping my feelings hostage but this time I must let this little butterfly free.

We're starting off on an ok note. It's very cold as per, and I decided to do something different for my birthday this year. I'm treating myself with a photoshoot. Yes, I know it's something out of the norm, but why not? This year is going to be one to remember. Since I mentioned it's so cold out and I haven't been away since 2018, Venti let's take a trip to St. Thomas and visit our family. It's been a while so pack your bags and don't forget to get tested before boarding the flight. Yup, that's the new norm around here. We must get tested before doing anything in today's world!

WOW!!! Venti thank you so much for accompanying me and experiencing such mind-blowing, picture postcard moments in these beautiful islands. Not only did we have the pleasure to visit St. Thomas and see family but we had the opportunity to visit other islands near it as well. Now it's time to bundle up and head back to Jack Frost and prepare us to celebrate Lily's birthday. Venti, I apologize for not mentioning Lily before, but she's my mother that has been battling cancer for three years and every birthday we've celebrated has been a blessing for us. I won't get too mushy with you Venti but you are more than welcome to join us for her dinner.

"... HAPPY BIRTHDAY DEAR LILY, HAPPY BIRTHDAY TO YOU!!!" Venti I am

beyond grateful for you being here and cherishing this moment with Lily. Even though her health has been slowly deteriorating, just seeing her smile lights up the dark room, it makes me intentionally become selfish and forget the pain she's really experiencing inside. Now that you've met her, Venti, please keep an eye on her while I'm busy with other things in life.

Sorry for the extra early text Venti, I know it's 6 am on this muggy May morning but a real close friend of mine has been shot and didn't make it. I know you haven't heard from me since Lily's birthday back in February, but I've been keeping to myself due to her health worsening, and my focus has been strictly on her. Please don't abandon me, Venti; you're the only person I feel comfortable venting to since my best friend just moved to Florida. Lily has had several procedures done to attempt to prolong her life. Everything around me has been happening so fast. Venti, for every positive step we take, I feel like I'm getting tested with a pile of negative challenges. Seeing another friend in a casket is not something I'm prepared to experience now. Please get back to me when you read this!

Hey Venti, it's me again, I'm not sure if you received my last message, and I sure don't remember if I mentioned that my Bry Bry aka my little mermaid aka my goddaughter, is graduating high school today! I probably didn't because I was going through it; sorry for rambling about all the bad things occurring at the time. But today we celebrate, and the best part about it is that she's only 16 years old and a junior in high school. In a few weeks, I'm taking her to St. Thomas since, of course, it's our last-minute planning graduation gift, but why not experience the beautiful views again. By the way, you're more than welcome to join me again. Talk to you soon!

"SURPRISE!!!" Venti sorry if you can't hear me, but we came down to Florida to surprise my best friend for his birthday. Yeah, he really thought that he was going to celebrate this year by his lonesome, but no Venti, no, he's not. It's a bittersweet vacation in the sunshine state because we're not hanging out like we expected to. Lily has once again been admitted to the hospital. I'll try my best to enjoy myself since I promised her that, but it's tough since for the first time in three years, I'm not physically there with her while she's fighting. On the bright side, September is next month, Venti, and that means I'm going to stand at the altar next to one of my brothers, as he marries his love.

Venti are you there? Remember how I kindly asked you to watch over Lily while I wasn't present? Well, I don't think you've been doing a good job at it because now she's at home counting her days. She hasn't been eating nor speaking much, and I don't know if I should blame you or blame myself for taking it too lightly when she was doing good? Or maybe I should blame science for not doing enough and maybe her higher power for allowing a person like her to go through such a thing. Ugh, I'm so *BLEEPING* upset ... I HATE YOU, VENTI!!!

... R.I.P. LILY ...

"5 ... 4 ... 3 ... 2 ... 1 ... HAPPY NEW YEAR!" WAIT!!! We can't end the year like this. First, I didn't know you were going to be at this New Year's Eve Party, Venti. I haven't spoken to you since last September. My mom was relieved from her pain. I apologize for taking my frustration out on you. I shouldn't have done that. Right before her passing, I was finally hired to work for the Department of Education, and guess what, Venti? Lily remembered that!!! Yes, her passing was extremely difficult for all of us, we all are mourning differently, but at least we're still here for one another. I'm proud of myself, Venti, for having the strength to not go back into a dark place like I did in the past after my grandfather's passing. I remembered everything an old friend of mine, ironically named Experience, taught me. My friend taught me how to take the bad and turn it into all the good that should be coming to me. Venti, this year I stumbled a lot but for every stumble, I was able to get up and keep going. You also taught me that at the beginning of the year. After a difficult September, I kept my head up. I remembered everything I learned, and with that, I was able to launch my latest clothing collection (which by the way, almost sold out before the launch) named REBIRTH. I also made a deal with Dr. Marten, the shoe company, to sponsor the shoot. As I mentioned before, I'm working at my old elementary school while still achieving my goals with my company. Venti, everything is falling into place, and I want to thank you for not leaving my side, even when you should have, due to my selfish behavior. On that note, I would like to end this year with a thank you and a cheer for all the memories and lessons learned.

Sincerely,
Me

P.S. Venti, we're still dealing with a lot of confusion about the new norm of Covid-19. A lot of back-and-forth information is being thrown at us. Everyone must be vaccinated, even the sharks and other sea creatures, lol. So please, Venti please tell your sibling to watch over us in this upcoming year. We need the best guidance possible!

letter 12

Dear 2021,

As I sit here, pondering about your younger self, I see that you have made me a stronger person. What do I mean by a stronger person? Glad you asked!

As opposed to the younger version of you, the you now made me realize that everything that matters starts and ends with my home. My home is my happy place, my haven, the only place that gets to see the real me. I am giddy with excitement every time I open the door, and my baby comes to greet me, or knowing that I will not be leaving their side for a whole two days. Sarcasm? You bet ya!

I feel like I have a lot to thank you for. You've made me understand that it is okay not to be perfect or to not work the hardest or to be everywhere for everyone. You've made me realize that I need to be next to them as much as possible because these days are counted, and they are passing by fast.

You've taught me to leave people where they are. If I don't talk to somebody for three months because I am consumed with my own life and them with their own, it's okay. Everyone is running their own race, and life keeps going. Before, I would question the distance, but now, too busy thinking of chores around the house, what my next move is going to be, or just what I am going to cook for my family.

You've also taught me that, while everyone is moving at 100mph, it is perfectly fine for me to move at a much slower pace. At this stage of my life, I want quality over quantity. The next move I make will be the best one for me and my family. Whatever move that is will be sweeter because I am practicing self-control by not listening to the noise and remaining true to myself—calculating, thinking five steps ahead, and thinking five years ahead. This right here, this very moment, as I hold my baby as he tries to go back to sleep at 3:04 am on a Tuesday, is where I want to be and where I need to be. This very moment wouldn't be possible if it wasn't for the planning and dedication I did to get to this point in my life.

Another thing you've taught me is to be more present! Present in the moment and not think about everything outside of that moment. So many things can rob me of my joy, such as work, my own family, things that my friends are dealing with, and cruel things around the world. The two people that I come home to every day bring the best out of me, and I would rob myself of creating memories with them if I concerned with anything outside of my home.

Lastly, you've taught me to appreciate. Appreciate my wife, son, mother, friends, and freedom to do what I do for a living. My wife is the pressure that stays in the back of my mind when I think I can't do something. My son looks at me like I am his superhero and protector. My momma, you know Dominican mamas and their grandkids, don't need to get into that. My boys and support system. Borrowing a cliché, what's understood by us doesn't need to be spoken.

Lastly, my service to help lights that fire to see the good in people even when they can't see it themselves.

I like how you treated me and the lessons you taught me. The little bit less mature, you, not so much, but he's in the past, and here we are. Thank you for listening to me. It means a lot to that you just let me process our relationship. Until we meet again, my dear friend!

Love,
Alcedito

> "The true marker of success in life is not what you have accomplished but what you've given."
> - Claudio E. Cabrera

letter 13

Greetings 2021,

It took a lot to gather the courage to write to you since I am still very bitter. I started the year hopeful because 2020 stole from myself and my loved ones. Things seemed to look up for a little while as mask mandates across the state started to ease, however, new fears were on the horizon. There were rumors that a vaccine mandate was going to be implemented to ensure the public safety of our nation. I was especially worried for my family, my job, and my students. And even with all of that, I still had to plan a wedding that was postponed over a year now.

One month I could invite 100 guests, another month I could invite 75 guests, and the numbers just kept increasing and decreasing. I was told that there would be a vaccine mandate for guests to attend my union. I was also told that only proof of a negative Covid test was needed for my guests. I just wanted to give up on the whole thing because I had paid and bought everything I needed for this wedding the year prior. Trying to salvage everything to survive an extra year seemed like a stupid idea. I wasn't even sure if I would fit into my wedding dress for goodness sakes. I stared at that dress and its garment bag showing its ugly face at me every day since my wedding was canceled in April of 2020. All I wanted to do was start my life with my new husband, but the obstacles facing us seemed endless.

I guess you could sense my frustration because you started to behave and we were able to have our special day. I was very happy that day, but I couldn't help but feel sad for the family members and friends I had to disinvite because of the Covid mandates placed on catering halls. So yes, I am very bitter with you 2021 to a certain extent. I am well aware that in light of my personal struggles there were people struggling much more than me. I can be upset with you a little, and I will accept that. But in a way, I also want to thank you for helping me realize that I wasn't in the struggle alone. Thank you for all the fear, the hurt, and the love.

Regards,
A Frustrated Fiance

letter 14

2021,

You know you remind me of that quote from Goethe's Faust: "I am part of that force which wills forever evil and works forever good." And it is only at the very end that I realized that despite all the disappointments, and your attempts at willing evil, the good always wins, even if you do not want to.

I wanted to break up with you so many times before! But each time I tried to end our relationship, I went through a wave of emotions because we all hoped so much that you were going to be our savior from that horrible 2020.

To be honest, you were not that much better. In fact, at times, you revealed the worst and the best in all of us. I choose to part ways with you now, not because I hope 2022 is better or because I need a new year to save us, but because I got everything I needed from you. As I grew, we grew ways apart.

You really started off with a bang on January 6th. I was so upset but I guess you let us know how you were in charge from the beginning. Thank you for your honesty ... I guess? I mean, how dare you let anyone attack our government? Have we not suffered enough? Did you ever think of the sacrifices people made to uphold our Constitution and to protect Democracy? Do you remember those countless people who died for us to get to where we are? 2021, at times I felt like you reversed all the progress our ancestors made.

To make things worse, the attacks on Kabul airports took the lives of KIDS who were born almost the same time as we entered Afghanistan. I mean come on, 2021, some of them were just born in 2001. The loss of our service members in Kabul just made you so much more painful. How could you let that happen? I'm sorry, but you are also the 20th anniversary of 9/11 attacks and even though every single year is hard and will never be the same, you just reopened the wounds like no other year has.

You brought out a lot of hatred in people. I get it, you are going to try to blame 2020 for that, aren't you? See I was hoping that with your advent, people will finally learn that we all need to go the extra mile in times of crisis, but it actually went kind of the opposite way for some. People who made sacrifices with their lives and loved ones, for us to be here, did not look for scapegoats. So, why do I see so many people target others and blame innocent people for their misery? Sometimes I wonder if all you did 2021, was to wake us up and shake us up so we can stop being racist, xenophobic, homophobic and hateful and fight to preserve what we have. I wonder if you did all that to teach us how fragile our freedom is and what freedom actually means. Well, you have got a long way to go because some people are very confused about the definition of the word freedom. Maybe 2022 will do a better job than you.

Look 2021, let me give you some context why some of us might be getting a bit impatient: 1868 was the first time the word "equal" appeared in the U.S.Constitution. So, it took us a little less than 100 years to include that word in our Supreme Law of the Land. 2021, you are about 160 years older than the 14th Amendment, which brought that word to us, don't you think it's time you start having to practice equality? How long will it take for all the kids to have equal opportunity and access to be successful? How long is it going to take for everyone to have the opportunity to achieve their American Dream? How long will it take for everyone to be treated with equal respect and manners? How long will people realize not to listen to our ill-wishers and all the misinformation out there meant to harm us?

Despite all the bad things you did, I don't hold any grudges and I just want to part ways. What I learned is that I have no choice but to always be the bigger person. If I am not the bigger person, in any situation, as tiring as it is, I will abase myself to those doing the harm. I also learned that eventually, repeated kindness, no matter what, is contagious (or at least I keep convincing myself of it). And maybe it is not true, but I choose to adamantly believe in it because I have no choice. And you know what, for that 2021, I am so grateful to you, which is precisely why I am ready to part ways with you without any remorse or grudges.

Despite all the heartbreaking things, I also saw incredible acts of kindness from everyday people who choose to remain anonymous. People who did not help others for fame or any reward but helped because that is what you should do. I saw people start community refrigerators, share their bare resources with others, and put themselves at risk when they did not have to, to serve and protect others. And I hope you remember acts of courage, sacrifice, and service as you leave and not all those who tried to misinform and destroy our way of life. I saw people not walk by and ignore but fight for what is fair, just, and necessary, even if it was to their own detriment. Because you know what 2021? "Injustice anywhere," like MLK Jr. said, "is a threat to justice everywhere." So, take care 2021 and the good will win!

Goodbye,
Someone who loves NY

letter 15

Dear 2021,

You were one of the best years my life had given me.

I started the year already pregnant, finishing ultrasound school, and still working at Best Buy.

I was already happy, but you must have liked me because things got even better. When I went for my 12-week ultrasound, the supervisor scanned me, and somehow it came up that I was also a sonographer looking for a job, and a week later, I got hired for a job there. It is such an enormous privilege to work at one of the best hospitals in NYC.

Around July, my father had a stroke. He was unconscious in his living room for the entire night until my grandma found him. It was one of the scariest things because I wanted to freak out, but I couldn't because of the stress it would put on my princess. Luckily, my cousin, my savior, the family's rock, literally took over everything and made sure I stayed updated about my father's care. I even took a weekend trip to North Carolina. I'm happy that I did. My dad made it his goal to recover so that he could see his granddaughter.

Once I was back home, I went back to my regular schedule and life. My pregnancy was the most peaceful and happiest I've ever been in my entire life. I have no complaints, except for the heartburn. Because of how good I felt, I worked till I was 41 weeks pregnant. On August 17, I had to call out because I had contractions every 10 minutes. They were tolerable, and my nonstress test was good, so I declined when they offered to induce me. I wanted her to have a natural birth, so I went home. Around 1 am the next day, the contractions became more intense. I crawled on the floor, trying yoga moves and everything to calm myself and ease the pain down. It didn't work. I even tried a hot bath in hopes that it would make me feel better. Around 5 am I called the hospital, crying and begging them to get the baby out of me. The doctor asked me to come in and get an epidural (that's when the idea of going natural went out the window). My Mari-Novio (as I like to call him) came to pick me up, and my mom met us at the hospital.

Thirteen hours and a C-Section later, my baby, Ella, was here.

It was magical.

Even the sleepless nights and breastfeeding were magical.

And I'm so blessed that I didn't experience postpartum depression. I've seen what it does to women.

I will say, 2021, that things took a slight turn with you towards the end of the year. I did not mind that the family could not meet Ella; after all, we live in a new world, and with Covid still a thing, it's better to play it safe. But unfortunately, that wasn't all that was going wrong. In October, I got scammed for $4,000 from a so-called real estate agent who took advantage of me. It took me a while to get over this, but I believe there is always Karma. The cops couldn't do anything, and neither could the bank. It broke my heart that someone could do that to me, let alone my daughter because I worked tirelessly until 41 weeks of pregnancy to make sure I had something in my savings in case of an emergency. My only consolation is that in the end, they will get what they deserve.

December rolled in, and I could not help but feel grateful. I shifted my focus from the negative things and decided to focus all my energy on all the good you had given me instead. My daughter and I received nonstop blessings from you. Yes, we had loss in the family; my dad had fallen ill and I lost money. However, even with those devastations, I still have my daughter with me. I have family, I have support, and I have love. And you kept on blessing me till the end. On the last week of the year, the very last couple of days of your stay, we got yet another blessing. My little family and I finally got a place to call home, A home where we can be together, grow, and create new memories.

I look forward to every day. I am excited for what's yet to come.

If I could, I would never have wanted 2021 to end. You were just that good to me. The blessings outnumbered the heartaches. You are a year I will never forget. I don't think I could ever break up with you. You will live forever in my heart.

I will miss you forever.

Love, Clara

.

letter 16

Dear 2021,

As I laid in bed last night, on your last day, to reflect on what you actually contributed to my life, I legit couldn't even remember how you started. What I did on January 1, 2021, is a complete mystery in my memory bank. I was lucky enough to find a picture I took on the night of your eve, so at least I know I stepped out in hopes of celebrating you. 2020 had left huge wounds for you to heal and plenty of pieces for you to put back together, and quite frankly ... You failed! Forgettable is rather modest, for what you truly were to me ... if I could explain it best, I'd say you were 2020 with a disguise. The real "2020 too." You did nothing different. You did nothing better ... you continued to wound, destroy and separate people, lives, businesses, everything. 2021, your continuation of misery and meek attempt at restoring what we lost in 2020, was quite embarrassing ... If "I'm just here so I don't get fired" was a year, you'd take the grand prize.

And even so, I thank you and dismiss you with honor. Because all that I searched for in you for 365 days, you managed to give me in your last couple of hours. You brought me clarity, encouragement, and a genuine and magnificent breakthrough. Your misery and failure have taught me to rely on ME and not you or the other years to come. I am fully responsible for what I did or didn't make of you and what I'll make of 2022.

Best Regards,
MARYposa

letter 17

Dear 2021,

I am very grateful to have had your friendship, but I do not want to continue being your friend anymore. You brought me good things, but also, and mostly, bad things. Let me tell you some of the reasons why I think we should stop being friends.

At the beginning of our friendship, it was the second year of the pandemic, and we were in virtual classes. Although virtual classes are not the worst, I do not think that a good friend would make me go through that. Virtual classes were stressful and confusing at times and having to do all my schoolwork on a computer was overwhelming. Not being able to socialize with my classmates was very disappointing. I wanted to see my friends in person, and you did not let me.

In virtual school, the lessons were more complicated than in the classroom, and honestly, I did not learn much because there was always some issue with the technology. There was always something that was going wrong. Also, virtual classes made it easy for students to cheat. Taking virtual tests was so annoying, but it was even more annoying because I knew that some students who were never in class and never put in the same effort would come and cheat and get a good grade. If the teachers left you alone with an exam on a computer with internet access, what do you think these kids were going to do? It wasn't fair to the kids who did their work without cheating and always paid attention. The ones that never did their work on time and cheated on tests got the same score and that made me feel very discouraged. I even started thinking if it even mattered for me to do all the work, but that just isn't me. I like school, and I take pride in my work, so I just continued to do my work and try my best.

After a while 2021, I understood that everyone was going to get a good grade just for putting in the effort, and though I did not agree with it, I think I know why you did it. It was to help the families that were having a hard time. Virtual classes had many conflicts, but they were the best for everyone's health. But thank you because eventually, your friendship brought me back to in-person classes. I'm not going to lie; at first, being back at school was a bit scary because we didn't know what the new rules would be like and what it would be like to wear masks all day, but in the end, everything went well when we all did our part to get back to normal.

We had to wear masks all day. We also had to stay six feet away or more from our friends and do Covid-19 tests at school. A lot had changed. We had to disinfect everything that was used in the classroom and wash our hands every time we entered and left the room. We couldn't even go on school trips or have classroom parties and that was so frustrating. But the most frustrating thing was that some kids did not know how to do some things because they had not been paying attention in virtual classes. This made all of us students look bad, and the teacher was clearly frustrated. She thought that absolutely all of us were the same and we did not do our part to learn in virtual classes.

2021, another reason why we should stop being friends is because of how you made me stay away from the people I love. Because we were still afraid to leave home, I lost friends and could only see my family through an electronic device.

Not leaving the house was very frustrating, and I began to prefer staying at home to having to go out and wear a mask all the time. To have to stay at home for the second year even made me not like going out anymore. In the beginning, I wanted so much to be able to go out, but now, I like staying home and don't really care anymore. I prefer staying in.

Another thing that made me angry with you was the distance. Having to keep a distance from the people I love made me lose friends. Not being able to visit them and only being able to talk to them through an electronic device makes people distance themselves. I only hoped that you would be different. I thought that after a whole year of the pandemic, you were going to change, but it was not like that. I hoped that you would make us all return to normality and recover those people that we lost because of distance and that maybe we would all go back to being like before, and maybe you did it a little bit, but it wasn't as I expected it to be. I thought you were the friend who was going to fix everything completely, but it wasn't like that and although you weren't the worst friend I've ever had your friendship disappointed me.

Although you weren't the best friend I've ever had, you weren't the worst either. Your friendship led me to meet new people and understand that it was difficult for everyone. Your friendship taught me to appreciate things more and to know that even though now is a bad time, in the end, bad times are not forever and pass. I am very grateful for having had your friendship.

Goodbye 2021, and thank you for everything.

Carmen, a frustrated but grateful
5th-grade student

letter 18

Dear 2021,

How can I talk to you without first mentioning 2020? Don't worry, I won't take away from your spotlight, but I will say this, because of everything that 2020 took away from me, I was determined to make you better. After almost a whole year of not traveling because of the pandemic, I was finally able to travel and celebrate my 33rd birthday at Disney World in December. It was magical. After that trip, it was as if Pandora's Box was opened for my fiancé and me. Within the year, you allowed me to take flights, visit islands, and experience places that I hadn't been able to because they were too expensive pre-pandemic. Now inexpensive and accessible to us, we made it our mission to make you one of the best years of our life together and not let any pandemic ruin what we had planned or live in fear of the unknown.

Our goal was to either travel monthly or experience something spectacular every month. We visited Miami with my sister and nephew for a beautiful relaxing week by the beach in January. Working remotely and being able to see the beach on my lunch break was one of the highlights of that month. In February, we visited Aruba during winter break for the first time in our lives. One happy island it truly is. The beautiful sunsets, warm ocean water, and amazing people make it an unforgettable paradise! We spent a fun-filled weekend in Cancun, Mexico, during spring break at the end of March. Hopping on a catamaran and visiting different islands in the country was the highlight of that month after working straight for weeks. We didn't catch a flight in April, but we did spend a weekend at the airport. A staycation at the TWA hotel to celebrate our 12th anniversary together was just the refresh we needed. Enjoying the heated infinity pool on the rooftop and watching the planes take off & land was indeed an amazing experience. In May, during Memorial Day weekend, we flew to Bonao, Dominican Republic, to lay a king to rest. Our days were filled with reuniting with family and celebrating life to the fullest. Filled with laughter and most importantly, with love.

On June 28th, two days after the 2020-2021 school year ended, we escaped to the Bahamas and spent our days relaxing at the Atlantis Paradise Island resort. There, the daily aquarium walks and going down thrilling water park water slides filled our days. We returned a few days into July to begin what would be an adventure-filled summer.

July was spent visiting museums, catching games at Yankee Stadium, and even seeing Space Jam 2 in theaters. In August, we celebrated my fiancé's 38th birthday by having a cigar room-themed super party in the park near our house with our closest friends and family. We had a cigar roller for everyone's pleasure, good food, and, of course, the drinks were flowing. A summer night to remember for sure!

In September, we visited Disney's Animal Kingdom in Florida to see he World of Avatar and ride through the Kilimanjaro Safari. We also celebrated with family members we hadn't seen since before the pandemic at my little cousin's Sweet 16 down in Port Saint Lucie. My family sure does know how to party. In October, Broadway was back in theaters, and so were we. Seeing the Lion King for the second time since we've been together and visiting Proud Rock is just as amazing as experiencing a beautiful island. We also took a trip on the magic carpet in Aladdin on Broadway during October, which is as magical as taking a smooth plane ride over the Atlantic Ocean. In November, we made final plans for our 2022 wedding that we are so over the moon about. In early December, I was able to go back down to Fort Lauderdale, Florida, to surprise my cousin at her baby shower with my parents for the weekend. Nothing fills my heart more than spending time with them. For my 34th birthday in December, my fiancé and I traveled to Costa Rica. A mix of relaxation and adventure filled our days. The country is beautiful, and the people are so welcoming. We got the experience of hot springs, something I've wanted to do for years. We zip-lined through the jungle with amazing views of the Arenal volcano. Indeed, an unforgettable time. Getting back home was an adventure in itself. We experienced two canceled flights home and had to ring in the New Year in a hotel shuttle in North Carolina.

2021 I wouldn't change you for the world. You brought my fiancé and me closer than ever, and for that, I am forever grateful for you!

Thank you for the experiences, the highs, the lows, and the incredible blessings! I'm forever indebted to you for the foundation my fiancé and I were able to build this year.

Sincerely,
Stephanie Valdez, soon to be Colon
(Wedding date 2.22.22)

letter 19

Dear 2021,

Still, still recovering from the aftermath of 2020. I promised to get a hold of myself this year, to finally put myself first, in every way possible. This was supposed to be my year. I dedicated the first half of 2021 to finishing up my last semester in grad school, completing internship hours, looking for jobs as a mental health therapist, and working a job that took a toll on me physically and mentally. It felt surreal to know that I would finally be done with school. The first six months were hectic, but personal development and growth happened.

In May 2021, I graduated with my degree in Mental Health Counseling. Due to the pandemic, I did not get to walk. Probably the only graduation I ever cared for, and I did not get to experience it. This victory was personal, but you stole the celebration. In 2020, I remember thinking to myself, "This pandemic won't last long; as long as it is over before I graduate, I'm fine," but Covid-19 had other plans. I remember feeling so gloomy on my graduation day because I would not get the chance to walk up on that stage and collect the diploma I worked so hard for. The only thing I had to look forward to was celebrating with my friends and family, but it was not fulfilling. A month before graduating, I started applying to jobs and had several offers to be a therapist. I could not believe this was happening so fast. I thought obtaining a job in my field would be a process.

I set a deadline for myself. I was determined to quit my job before October with or without a second option. I refused to enter a birthday in misery. My job at the time was mentally draining, and I had to let it go regardless of what life would hand me. Because honestly, what therapist would I be to advocate for self-happiness but not practice it myself? Lucky for me, I landed a job within the timeframe I set for myself. I was hired as a bilingual Mental Health Therapist, and I honestly could not be more excited. Anxious. Overwhelmed. Shocked. I finally achieved my dreams.

My dream to help people heal through their troubles. But what healing can I do if I'm still a work in progress? Accepting this opportunity meant some deep reflection had to be done to explore inner wounds, and understand my own thoughts, behaviors, and emotions. Earning my degree was a personal journey.

But what happens next when you have achieved your biggest dream? Do you continue to dream? It may feel like I've accomplished it all, but now I ask myself, what happens next? This was supposed to be my year, but why do I not feel fulfilled? Why do I need more? What happens next? Where do I go from here? Is my next dream to find love? Would that truly be me or just filling in society's standards? An intrusive thought I struggle with daily. Everyone is always asking about my personal life. It's as if a woman who obtained higher education and achieved her dream job cannot exist without love. I've always felt that love comes on its own; there's no need to search for it. But the questions people present are triggering. I do not know why I let it get to me. I know that whatever is meant to happen next will.

I find myself sitting in confusion because I just don't know what happens next. The last six months of 2021 were a constant battle of "I made it" and "I'm not doing good enough." I am my biggest competitor and critic. You 2021 taught me that I struggle with being confident in my decision-making, I struggle to stand against intrusive thoughts, and I struggle to be content with who I am. It's a battle of me vs. me.

As a therapist, I understand that being my own critic will only inhibit my growth. But I can't help but feel that I have not accomplished much if my accomplishments are measured by a piece of fancy paper that states my name and degree.

With you 2021, I found myself stuck. My life felt stuck, and even when I had it all planned out, it just felt so unsettled. I felt changes happening within me, my personality was changing, but the changes felt positive, but the feeling was unfamiliar. It's like I was growing into myself. I felt myself craving isolation, just wanting to be left alone in my thoughts. Everything I did felt like a task, talking to my friends, checking in on people, making time for them all felt forced. But sometimes, those moments keep you going. That alone time allowed me to explore parts of myself I didn't know existed.

All I hope for in 2022 is to find self-awareness and practice self-kindness, continue to heal myself and others, and experience the world differently.

Goodbye 2021, it's been a ride.

Sincerely,
Your favorite therapist,
Julyssa

letter 20

Dear 2021,

We learned a lot from you, but I think you were just a continuation of 2020, maybe except towards the end.

Many of us were still having a tough time adjusting to being online and everything changing around us. It was a very sudden change, and while some adapted reasonably well, others, like me, just couldn't adjust to a different type of learning so fast. School online was very challenging because it was not the same as being in the classroom. We missed our friend's jokes and believe it or not, seeing our teacher's faces. Remote took all of that away from us. We could not see anyone. Everyone just became a box on the screen, and I did not like being reduced to that. I missed the interactions with others, I missed being there in person.

I know that some had the opportunity to be in school during your time here, but not many were in the classrooms 100% of the time. We were still scared of what 2020 had unleashed, and the best solutions that schools could find were to have us attend in a blended format. Some days we were in school, and on others, we had to stay remote to avoid large groups in the classroom. Some parents also had the option of keeping their kids home 100% of the time. Yes, we were hoping that your solutions could be helpful, and we were all looking forward to seeing our friends and teachers and leaving our homes, but you were a tough one to deal with. Blended learning, with some days in the classroom and some online, was too confusing. I had some days online, and I was just tired of it. I had difficulty focusing; looking at a screen for hours was exhausting. I didn't even have a good relationship with my teachers because I rarely saw them. How am I supposed to build relationships with people I cannot see long enough for them to see the real me? I was not used to this, so adjusting to this new learning environment became extremely hard.

I wish I could say that at least I had friends to talk to, but as a freshman starting the year remote in a new school, the situation was not ideal for making friends. Friendships that could have started with a simple question like "Can I borrow a pencil?" were out of the question. There is none of that online. So, making friends was the worst. Trying to speak to someone you have never seen and know nothing about was complicated and weird.

Fortunately, once the vaccine came out, things started to look bright, and my sophomore year was beginning to look great. You changed the rules for the new school year, everyone could get back to school in person, and I mean everyone! Thank you. There were no more online classes; I was going to finally meet my teachers face to face once and for all and start making friends. I met my amazing teachers and two of my closest friends, and this was great because I finally got to interact with others in the classroom and do all the things that I was missing from the last school year. It felt amazing.

As time passed, you allowed us the chance to start playing sports again, and that was really fun. Being on a team again and hanging out with my coach and teammates was exciting. I was now creating the memories I had missed from the prior year. Making jokes in the classroom and the gym, finally working in groups and doing the things we hadn't done in a while. My school had also planned a trip with the first-year students, it was like everything was going back to normal. Everything was back to normal besides wearing a mask, but that was the last of my worries. Everything looked bright, no more lockdown and definitely no more online school. I was able to gather with my friends and go places like the park or the theaters, and we became so close.

Overall 2021, you were tough to be around, but eventually, with time, you weren't. It was great being with you, but I think it's time to move on to better things.

With love,
Gabbs
(A grateful HS Sophomore)

letter 21

Dear 2021,

We started with so much promise. I didn't bring in the baggage from my past relationship with 2020, although it did leave me rather damaged and traumatized. I was still recovering with you, but I convinced myself that my next relationship would not scar me as much as my last one. Unfortunately, early on, I saw some significant similarities. You kept me away from my dad, who was sick and needed me, just like 2020 kept me from my mom in her final days. I can never forgive you for what you've done, for making me a liar when I told my dad I would see him on Wednesday after work because you took him from me that same day before my workday was over. I'll never forget the pain I felt on a day that was supposed to be like any other, a pain so deep that I tried to hold in because I wanted to seem professional, but I was so overcome with emotion and anger that I broke down in my office. The person who appears to have it together, who can manage her feelings, the person who helps everyone else when they are falling apart now became the person who couldn't hold it together and needed comfort from others. This was a new vulnerable me that I was allowing others to see, and it was as uncomfortable as it was comforting to allow myself just to feel what I was feeling in the moment.

You tried to rob me of my peace and sanity. You filled my body with pain and sorrow so deep I was scared even to address what I was feeling. I had just dealt with the loss of my mom and being there for my dad helped me channel my energy and keep my mind occupied. But you took that from me too. You wanted to leave me feeling like I had nothing, and you almost succeeded. I often would lay awake at night thinking about all the things I wish I had said and wished I had done differently but that only made me feel worse because the fact remained that my hands were tied because of you. You somehow managed to keep a hold of me even when I was over you, and I swore that you would no longer get the best of me.

I never thought of myself as the type of person to let someone else control my emotions or my happiness, but I lost myself in you for a long time. While I hate you for what you took from me, I admit that it wasn't until I was at my lowest point and felt I had nothing left to lose that I realized that if I don't love myself, I have truly let you defeat me. I refuse to give you any more of my power, energy, or strength. It was you causing my life to go into a tailspin that actually helped me become stronger because, for the first time in a very long time in my life, I remembered that I needed time to care for myself. I realized I needed to provide the love, care, and nurturing I provide to others to myself.

Because of all this tragedy and loss, I have developed a new appreciation for myself. My well-being is now my priority. I have started to focus on myself, eating better, exercising (although I could do better), losing over 50 pounds, and have even started dating again. I am not settling anymore. I want to seek out my happiness and enjoy it while I have it. I know that our time on this earth is not infinite, and we should make the best of it while we have life to live. I want to live with no more regrets. I want to feel free and accept the love I have around me. You took my loved ones, but you didn't take away all my love. I feel fortunate and appreciative of the people in my life who have always been there for me, and I realized that family is not just those to who you are genetically related to. My support system is strong, and you can't penetrate that.

So, 2021, I first want to say fuck you for robbing me of more time with my father, fuck you for the depression, the insecurities, the feelings of despair and hopelessness. But I also want to close by saying thank you. In your efforts to ruin me, you have actually helped me find myself again. Your plan backfired. I am not a mess anymore. I am now someone who has nothing left but hope and promise. My mindset has shifted, and I want to live life to the fullest and continue to work on loving and respecting myself while on my search for happiness. Gone are the days of Laura's life only revolving around caring for others. Today Laura is the priority, and Laura is done talking about you, 2021.

You are old news.

Good riddance!

I hope to never hear from you again or experience another relationship like the one we had!

Laura

space for your own

Lissedia Batista-Gonzalez was born and raised in The Dominican Republic until the age of 11. In the Summer of 1995, she and her two younger siblings moved to New York City to live with their parents, who already lived in the US and worked hard to bring their children and provide them with better opportunities. Ms. Batista-Gonzalez discovered a passion for teaching at an early age when she was an active participant in a community-based program that offered mentorship and education to youths of low-income families. She holds a Bachelor's in Arts in Foreign Language and a Master's of Science in Special Education. She lives with her husband and three children in the same community she now serves. Dear 2021: 21 Letters for 2021 is her second book. She Self-published her first book of a similar title, Dear 2020: 20 Letters for 2020, in March of 2021.

126

Made in the USA
Middletown, DE
07 July 2022

68750331R00076